A Bird Lover's STICKER BOOK

ILLUSTRATED BY LEANA FISCHER

Workman Publishing · New York

Workman
Workman Publishing
Hachette Book Group, Inc.
1290 Avenue of the Americas
New York, NY 10104
workman.com

Workman is an imprint of Workman Publishing, a division of Hachette Book Group, Inc. The Workman name and logo are registered trademarks of Hachette Book Group, Inc.

Cover design by Rae Ann Spitzenberger
Watercolor wash (cover, title page, p. 72) © TairA/Shutterstock

The publisher is not responsible for websites (or their content) that are not owned by the publisher.

Workman books may be purchased in bulk for business, educational, or promotional use. For information, please contact your local bookseller or the Hachette Book Group Special Markets Department at special.markets@hbgusa.com.

ISBN 978-1-5235-2448-8

First Edition April 2024

Printed in China on responsibly sourced paper.

10 9 8 7 6 5 4 3 2 1

LET YOUR IMAGINATION TAKE FLIGHT as you soar into the colorful world of birds! Packed with more than 675 stickers, this lushly illustrated sticker book will take you on a bird-watching adventure from your own backyard to the peaks of majestic mountains and everywhere in between. Flit among the branches of a cherry tree with cardinals, blue jays, and titmice; glide with Canada geese across a flower-dotted prairie; and swim with playful penguins in the Arctic.

Whether you're a seasoned nature lover or simply looking to add some beauty to your day, these charming stickers will add a delightful touch to your journals, letters, notebooks, postcards, and anything else you can imagine. So break out your binoculars–it's time to step into these magical habitats and discover beautiful birds around every corner.

Little
by little,
the bird
builds
its nest.

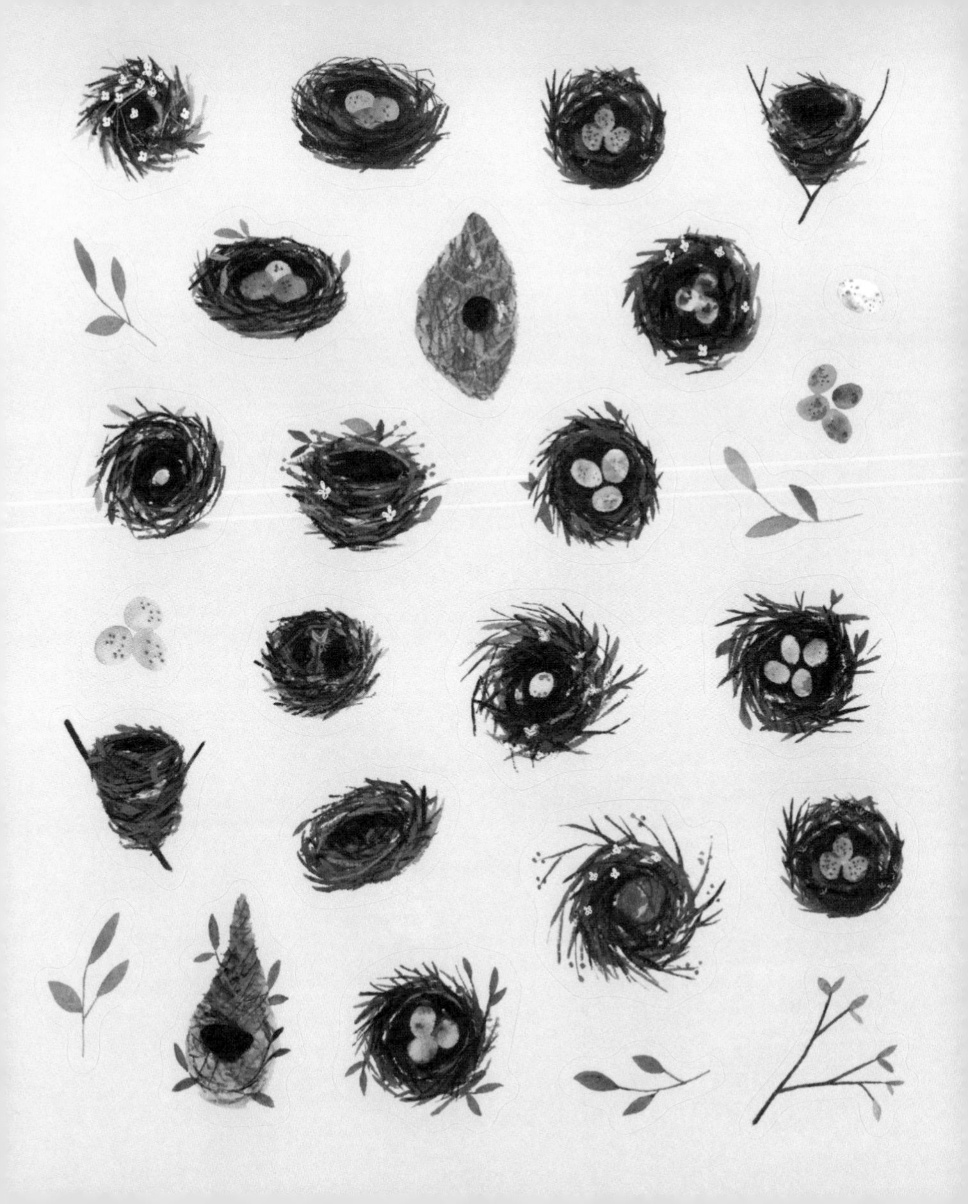

As the crow flies.

Birds
of a
feather.

ABOUT THE ILLUSTRATOR

Each beak, feather, and flower was lovingly illustrated by Leana Fischer, the watercolor artist behind the stationery company May We Fly. She teaches in-person and online watercolor workshops and has partnered with brands such as Terrain, Trader Joe's, and Hallmark. In 2019, she completed a 100-Day Project in which she painted every state bird and flower. Leana lives in the Blue Ridge Mountains of Virginia, where she works and paints out of her home studio. The bird feeder outside her studio window brought lots of visitors who inspired her and kept her company during the process of creating this book. She hopes these feathered friends will bring as much joy to your world as they did to hers. To see more of Leana's work, visit maywefly.com.

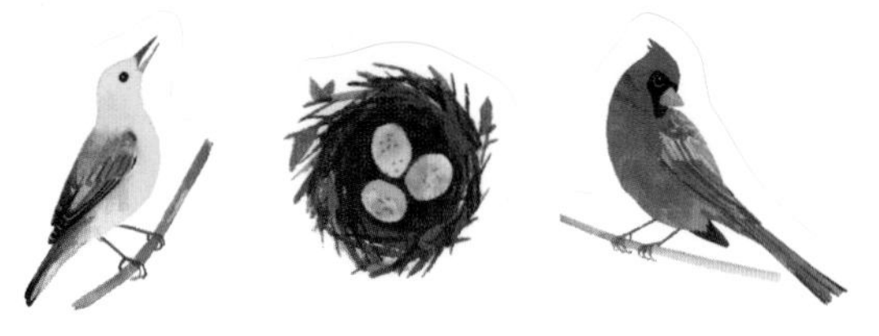